Praise for Teaching Diamonds in the Tough

Teaching Diamonds in the Tough is a great read for anybody who wants to work in education in the city. Lampos writes contextually with an excitement to shape not just the minds of children, but their character. Her "look it up," "chalk it up" segments are relevant and will be useful for years to come. I'm excited to see how and where her book influences future Christian educators.

Pastor Joe Huizenga,
Roseland Christian Ministries, Chicago

Cleo shares personal and professional conviction with both wit and passion born of dedicated experience. The beauty of her optimism enlightens the shadows of our reality, and we are enriched by her gifts to us.

Dr. Erv Barnes, PhD.
Author, Educator, Advocate

Teaching Diamonds in the Tough is an inspiring and uplifting, yet sometimes disheartening examination of teaching in a poverty-ridden school and all the problems associated with it. As an urban teacher, these beautifully written vignettes took me back to the classroom, experiencing once again the exhuberance and joys of teaching as well as the sadness and frustration that left me drained at the end of the day. Both veteran and novice teachers will benefit from Cleo Lampos' unique perspective.

Frank Victoria, retired
Chicago Public School teacher and author

Cleo Lampos' heart for children and ability to see the potential in the most problematic child makes this book an inspiring and practical read for discouraged teachers.

Addie Mix, Co-founder of
RAY, Reclaim A Youth

A warm reminder that God works unexpectedly and that He uses us to touch others through even the smallest gestures of kindness.

Mary Byers, author, The Mother Load:
How to Meet Your Own
Needs While Caring For Your Family.

Teaching Diamonds in the Tough captures the essence of the difficulties and mood of children in the inner city who face poverty, drugs and gangs every day. This book is a must read for teachers everywhere.

Maggie McInerney,
Middle School Teacher, Chicago

The stories and lesson plans show how imperative it is for teachers to be sensitive to the hurt, pain and fears of these children. Your stories are heart rending. Sensitivity, hope and love are critical components of reaching the student. Your lesson plans beautifully address the issues!

Marilyn Mulder, B.M.Ed; M.M.
Organ, Trinity Christian College, Palos Heights, IL

We live in an urbanized world. The effects show up in America's classrooms whether they are urban or rural. Teachers need nurture, encouragement, inspiration and, yes, food for their faith. Cleo Lampos has provided these in great supply in *Teaching Diamonds in the Tough*.

Pastor Charles Lyons,
Armitage Church, Chicago

Cleo has great insight into what it is to teach special needs children and a wonderful message into what is learned from teaching these special education students. Short, encouraging chapters that are both challenging and inspiring.

Betsy Retsema, Second Grade Teacher,
Southwest Christian School, Oak Lawn, Illinois

Cleo Lampos' compassionate heart finds the hidden potential in children, while giving us a practical over-the-shoulder tutorial on effective teaching strategies.

Rich Rubietta, song writer, musician, educator,
Abounding Ministries, Grayslake, Il.

TEACHING DIAMONDS IN THE TOUGH:
MINING THE POTENTIAL IN EVERY STUDENT
BY CLEO LAMPOS
Published by Lighthouse Publishing of the Carolinas
2333 Barton Oaks Dr., Raleigh, NC, 27614

ISBN 978-1-938499-06-7

Available in print from your local bookstore, online, or from the publisher at: www.lighthousepublishingofthecarolinas.com

For more information on this book and the author visit:
http://www.facebook.com/cleo.lampos

Library of Congress Cataloging-in-Publication Data
Lampos, Cleo.
Teaching Diamonds in the Tough: Mining the Potential in Every Student / Cleo Lampos 1st ed.

Printed in the United States of America

Table of Contents

TEACHING DIAMONDS IN THE TOUGH

Mining the Potential in Every Student

By Cleo Lampos

This book is dedicated to:
Jane Rubietta, Lynn Austin and Joy Bocenagra,
my writer friends who never gave up,
and
teachers at Roseland Christian School in Chicago,
who live every day with the challenges of teaching.

INTRODUCTION

Millions of teachers today are confronted by a profession complicated by pressure for standardized test scores, paperwork, public outcry and dysfunctional families. In the midst of the classroom, the heartaches and potential of an individual child can easily be overlooked by a teacher in desperate need of hope and help for herself.

Teaching Diamonds in the Tough: Mining the Potential in Every Student offers anecdotal inspiration to educators. Using daily experiences gleaned from years of teaching, these vignettes provide keen insight into the reasons why teachers stay in the classroom and how to read the souls of the students. All names have been changed to protect confidentiality, except for Mellissa Schultz and Mae Erie. At the conclusion of each passage, three sections reinforce the message. Quotes from famous educators appear in the *"Chalk It Up"* section. *"Look It Up"* provides relevant Scripture verses, and *"Lesson Plan"* invites further reflection or personal application from the reader. This devotional book addresses real life issues in an original manner. This is solid food for the starving souls of teachers.

As an educator for the past thirty years, Lampos taught in preschool, public elementary school, diagnostic learning center, special education and in the church. Her last assignment was fourth grade in a school described as "an urban school in a suburban setting." A Master's in Learning Disabilities and Behavior/Emotional Disorders in conjunction with certifications in gang awareness, violence, drug prevention and current educational practices have prepared her to teach and write about high risk students who are really "Diamonds in the Tough."

Articles about education that Lampos has written have appeared in journals such an *Evangelizing Today's Child, Teachers in Focus, Teacher Interaction, Baptist Leader, Virtue,* and *Religious Teacher's Journal.* She has been a member of a writer's critique group for 19 years and attended Write to Publish. She earned the 2011 Semifinalist Genesis Award in Young Adult. **Grandpa's Remembering Book,** a family friendly book about Alzheimer's Disease, was published with illustrators Maralyn Dettmann and Rene' Clark. Lampos also contributed to **Writing So Heaven Will Be Different**.

In her free time, Lampos works with her husband for Share the Harvest, which supplies fresh garden produce to local food pantries. They volunteer once a week at the Bible League thrift store which supplies literature to the Philippines. Serving with the worship planning team at Calvin Christian Reformed Church challenges her writing skills as well as membership in the Oak Lawn Library Writer's Group. Ten grandchildren round out a week's activities.

MELISSA'S GIFT

M elissa joined the staff at a time when middle-aged or forty-something teachers dominated. The twenty-something rookie with three years of experience reminded many of us of our daughters. It was difficult to rein in maternal feelings for Melissa, but, to our amazement, she didn't need our protecting or mentoring.

Coming to the public school from a parochial setting, Melissa soon had her class in lock-step precision as they walked to lunch and gym. Somehow she spoke softly to twenty-five students who responded, maybe out of love. Their teacher dressed up for school: long skirts swishing, hair up, hair down, hair braided in an Eastern European style.

Melissa's room boasted learning centers in each corner that changed weekly, as did many of the bulletin boards. On Friday afternoons, Melissa's grandparents came to the classroom with home-baked goodies and worked individually with students on reading or math. After school, several students stayed to help wash the desktop and counters. Melissa's grandmother put up intricately designed bulletin boards she had used in her many years teaching in the Chicago public school system.

I stood at my door day after day, looking across the hall at Melissa, glowingly greeting her students each morning. She seldom voiced frustration about so many children's apathy toward education. Only a few of us knew she cried about the lack of progress that her under-privileged children made despite her efforts to stimulate their creativity and challenge their skills. To those in her care, Melissa presented a picture of love, beauty and concern.

"I used to be like that," I often thought, watching her. Twenty years of teaching had deadened my soul, but Melissa rekindled a spark of idealism inside me that flickered dimly. After leaving college, I had chosen to teach in the Chicago area, wanting to reach the culturally deprived, high-risk students; thinking one teacher could make a difference; hoping to change lives in a positive way. I believed that God placed me in my particular classroom with specific students for a reason that stretched into eternity. Watching Melissa, that idealistic feeling returned and grew, changing my attitudes and style of teaching from tired and negative to a daily opportunity to reach out. At mid-life, I felt energized.

Melissa taught for another year. In her third year, she married her best friend, Kevin, in a quiet ceremony, autumn leaves ablaze on the trees. They spent weekends on short trips to spots of natural beauty in neighboring states. Their honeymoon appeared endless.

I was sitting in the teachers' lounge sipping my morning caffeine, when a phone call came through. "Melissa and Kevin were killed in an automobile accident while returning from Michigan. Kevin was thrown from the car as it impacted another. Melissa burned in the driver's seat."

The social worker moved the crisis team into full counseling mode. Most of us pushed through personal pain to keep the situation calm. So many children, so many questions.

I had never been to a funeral with two caskets. Melissa and Kevin's wedding picture stood between the caskets, hundreds of flowers softening the brutal truth. We cried together as a faculty, we cried with the family, we cried until there were no more tears, only an ache in the heart. Melissa had accomplished much in a short time.

I still glance at Melissa's old room and remember her energy, concern, and desire to reach the most difficult student. And I thank God for placing Melissa in a particular classroom, in a specific school, so an old, apathetic teacher could rekindle her flame of passion for students.

Look It Up

"Take heed to the ministry which thou hast received in the Lord, that thou fulfill it."

Colossians 4:17

"Therefore, my beloved brethren, be ye steadfast, unmovable, always abounding in the work of the Lord, forasmuch as ye know that your labor is not in vain in the Lord."

I Corinthians 15:58

Chalk It Up

"Your life is destined to be an example. The only question is 'what kind?'"

–Marie T. Freeman

"Some people come into our lives and quietly go. Others stay for awhile and leave footprints on our hearts and we are never the same."

-Embroidered Motto on friend's wall

Lesson Plan

Think back to the reasons why becoming a teacher intrigued you. Get in touch with the idealism that motivated your dedication. Breathe your youth back into a tired body.

LOCK DOWN

Bewilderment covered Jenny's face. She mirrored my own expression. What was going on?

Thirty-year-old Jenny, a student-teacher/observer for the semester from a nearby university, knew children. Besides working at a pre-school to pay tuition, she was the mother of two. Only a few more hours in this reading class were needed to fulfill the thirty-hour requirement in language arts. But the behavior of the class this day puzzled both of us.

The reading class met for one hour each day. Fifteen students from all six fourth grades who achieved below ten percent on standardized tests but did not qualify for special education. All read below the second grade level. Gang member "wannabes." Lethargic learners. A thirteen year old waiting for parental signature for testing. Behavior problems. Home trauma. Anger. On any given day, at least one student was out on suspension. Jenny and I faced the challenges together, but could not figure out this latest problem.

"They've turned their backs on us," Jenny whispered from behind her hand. I nodded. "They won't answer any questions," she added. Another shake of my head. We stared at fourteen hunched backs, heads down. Body language heavy into rejection toward us. "They've distanced themselves from us."

Jenny's observation tapped some intuition inside me. "That's it, Jenny. They're mad. And they have every right to be angry at you, me, and the whole world. They're on emotional lock down."

Jenny's expression switched to total confusion. Taking Jenny to the back of the room, I explained. "Think of it, Jenny. Last week Melissa Schulz, a teacher, died in an auto accident. The death was sudden, unexpected. You know how these kids think teachers live and sleep at school. We are the constant in their life. The stability. They can count on us to be here, to care, to treat them fairly, and most importantly, not to walk out on them. Not to leave."

"This is their way of dealing with their abandonment issues. Don't get too close. Don't bond. Don't care. Then you'll never get hurt." I stopped so both of us could absorb the insight. Realization lit Jenny's face.

Eric's broad, thirteen-year-old shoulders were needed at home to be the "man of the house" for a mother who looked too young to be raising a teenager alone. Two foster children bent over their work sheets. DeShawn, whose grandmother raised him and his seven siblings while their mother wandered the streets in search of drugs. In the room, only three students lived in a two-parent family, all of them second marriages.

"Teachers aren't supposed to die. They aren't supposed to leave. The one stable place in these students' lives—school—is now shaky ground. Jenny, let's just take things easy today. Walk around. Talk with as many students as you can. Get eye contact. Don't let them shut us out."

We walked out among the desks. "How's it going, Eric?" I knelt by his desk, looking up into his deep brown eyes.

"Okay, Mrs. Lampos." He paused. "But I don't know this word, and I don't get question number six." He glanced over at me and our eyes met. A sadness from thirteen years of pain, the heaviness from a young heart, filled his face. But that day, Eric read. He read my soul.

I'm here. I won't leave by choice.

Look It Up

"I will never leave you nor forsake you."

Hebrews 13:5

Chalk It Up

"One sign of anxiety in children is an inability to easily make eye contact. An extremely anxious child will have problems approaching others, adults as well as peers. The emotionally deprived child will have difficulty in the simplest communication."

-Gary Chapman and Ross Campbell

Lesson Plan

Watch the behavior of the students in your class. Evaluate the behavior in terms of how it protects the student's emotions. Then, try to meet the perceived need.

THE MOURNING DOVE'S CRY

As part of my stress-reducing program, I sit on our patio in a black, wrought-iron rocking chair. The rhythm of my body releases the tightly held tension inside every fiber of muscle and nerve. The peacefulness of the wooden, fenced-in area is broken only by the sounds of early morning birds.

A thick evergreen tree by the garage twitters with activity, the long-needled branches swaying occasionally as some bird fluffs its feathers near the trunk. Blue jays dive in, carrying pieces of string or straw in their beaks for spring nest building. Little brown wrens flutter from the tree to the grapevine nearby in search of a crawly snack. Birds, whose names are unknown because I don't have a guide book to look them up, fly overhead and glide into Vern's garden for any wiggling treats unearthed by hoeing. The constant chatter among these feathered beings brings joyous peace to my spirits.

Then, from the overhanging eaves of our neighbor's lean-to, I detect a soft sound. Low, gentle, filled with sorrow. A mourning dove cries and the pain from its sound blends with a deep wound in my soul.

My rocking ceases as my ears focus on the softly weeping bird hidden by the eaves. A well of sorrow swells from the depths of my being to the surface. Tears spill from my eyes as thoughts flow through my mind. I mourn for the former student who aided in a brutal gang murder. For the ten year old who lived in a car. For the mother who died in a drug deal gone bad. For the dyslexic boy who tried so hard but found school to be a daily nightmare. For the small, skinny kid whom the others teased and bullied despite the teachers' interventions. For the girl with learning problems who was born with crack cocaine in her tiny body. For my own battles with hearing loss and mild stroke. Intellectually, I acknowledge that God promises "weeping is for the night, but joy comes in the morning."

But it is daybreak. On my cheeks a river of tears run. And as I listen to the dove's plaintive tones amid the lively chatter of the flock, I know.

I know why the mourning dove cries.

Look It Up

"Blessed are they that mourn; for they shall be comforted."

Matthew 5:4

Chalk It Up

"To be sure, I have seen trouble. I have had difficulty; the way has not been easy, but I have thanked God and said, "Glory Hallelujah!"

–Mary McLeod Bethune

"One of the great benefits to entering into one's grief, pain and loss is the ability to fully experience joy and abundant life after the mourning."

– Jane Rubietta

Lesson Plan

Try to remember that it is all right to mourn for losses. Think of the losses in your life that fill the heart with sorrow. Release them to the only one who can heal the broken hearted, and experience God's peace.

WONDERFUL WEDNESDAY

Homework Club exuded all the trappings of success. So it appeared on the surface. Fifteen students finished their assigned work before going home. Time ticked by quickly. The whole class rejoiced in that. So, why were the Homework Club members boring holes into me with their eyes? What could have gone wrong?

One more after-school responsibility had certainly not been my idea. Homework Club had long ago been excluded from my list of the committees worth volunteering my time and effort. At three o'clock, all energy drained from my body, so even extra pay could not entice me to tutor fifteen low-achieving students for an hour and a half. Only the assistant principal, Ms. Graham, could.

"Cleo. We need a teacher for the Wednesday afternoon Homework Club. The person who worked that assignment is teaching homebound students. Monday, Tuesday, and Thursday are covered. Can I count on you for Wednesday?" Ms. Graham smiled charmingly while she penciled my name in the schedule.

We breezed through the first session. The fourth grade students filed into my room. I knew many by reputation, either as non-readers or behavior problems. Using all the strategies gained from years in special education, I soon had each child working on individual assignments. Knowing that an energy boost helps, I passed out chocolate covered graham crackers. The early December snow floated from the gray clouds, covering the world in silent white drifts. Cozy inside, I tiptoed from desk to desk, trying an old technique in auditory spelling with one student, pairing others to teach alternate paragraphs from the same passage, getting a times tables sheet for computation to another.

"Can we stay overnight?" Travis asked.

"Yeah. We could order pizza," piped in Mike.

"We could put our coats on the floor to sleep," Katie added.

"I've got to get home to make supper for Mr. Lampos." Disappointed moans followed.

Just before the time to put on coats, boots and muffs, I told everyone to listen to our "goodbye song," a tape that my regular class knew as the cue to get ready for the weekend. It's an old rendition of "What A Wonderful World." In an easy-paced rhythm, Louis Armstrong's voice filled the room. *"I see skies of blue . . . and I say to myself, what a wonderful world."* I lip-synced and motioned the words with wide sweeps of my arms. *"Oh, yeah!"* The music faded.

I watched as the Homework Club donned their winter wraps in silence, then queued up into a sloppy line. Staring eyes and slack mouths made me ask, "What? Hey, guys, weren't you just listening? It's a wonderful world. How about some smiles?"

Preppy, well-dressed Thad cocked his head. "It's not a wonderful world, Mrs.. Lampos. My stepfather hates me. I don't like to go home." I envisioned Thad and a few other walkers standing by the front entrance on frigid mornings.

"I don't think it's such a wonderful world, either," snapped Travis whose father still served a prison term for gang-related offenses.

Grunts of confirmation surrounded me. Angry feelings vented through words.

"It's a lousy world."

"Life's no fun."

Stepping back into my childhood, memories of wanting to stay in school flooded my mind. Cautiously, I shared them with the Club.

"Believe it or not, I know how you feel. My stepfather was a mean alcoholic. There was a lot of fighting at my home. We were poor and sometimes hungry. School was safer and nicer than home."

Shock crossed their faces as I spoke.

"But I never let the bad things get me down. Even at your age, I looked around and tried to find the good things in life. That's why I like Louis Armstrong's song. Wonderful things are free, like the sky, babies smiling, the snow wrapping us up today in a hug. Your assignment for next Wednesday is to come to Homework Club with five wonderful things in your life. Can we do this?"

Upturned lips and nodding heads said it all. Several boys hugged me on the way to the bus. Surely God has made something very special for this midweek group, I reflected. Let it be His wonderful love flowing through me to these needy hearts.

Look It Up

"Finally, brethren, whatsoever things are true, whatsoever things are just, whatsoever things are pure, whatsoever things are lovely, whatsoever things are of good report; if there be any virtue, and if there be any praise, think on these things."

Philippians 4:8

Chalk It Up

"Loneliness and the feeling of being unwanted is the most terrible poverty."

-Mother Teresa

Lesson Plan

Help your students to contemplate the positive aspects of life. Make an "attitude of gratitude" list or bulletin board. Recap the week on Friday afternoon by stating all the positive things that happened. Remind them that this is a "wonderful world."

AN EXPLOSIVE SITUATION

The military cadence of hard sole shoes on tile floors broke the deathly silence of the detention room. Out of place in the empty corridors of afterschool, the crackling messages from walkie-talkies interrupted the rhythm of the marching feet. Eight pairs of eyes fixed questioningly on me. Neither myself nor the detention "regulars" recalled police in the halls this late in the afternoon.

The assistant principal beckoned to me from the door. The urgency on her face moved me rapidly to the other side of the room. With furtive whispers she explained, "The bus will be here in five minutes. Get the students ready. We need to evacuate now. There's a bomb somewhere." She strode back to the main office, leaving me stunned.

"Students. This is your lucky day. You get out of detention an hour early." The calm in my voice belied my quickening heartbeat." I managed a smile. "Gather your belongings. I'm anxious to get home, too." As the students packed their book bags, I grabbed my coat and purse.

Our hastily formed line passed more police in the halls, sweeping the school for explosives. On our way out of the double doors, the canine unit sniffed its way in. Blue lights flashed on ordinary cars lining the parkway. Off duty plain-clothed officers leaped from their vehicles and dashed along the sidewalk. Wide-eyed and speechless, the detention students boarded the bus, which sped out of the parking lot in a cloud of exhaust. The assistant principal indicated that all staff, too, should evacuate. By the time I had driven home, my head pounded with a stress related headache. Later the ten o'clock news reported that no explosives were found.

That night, I couldn't stop thinking about the fragility and capricious nature of life. My fate and those eight children rested on the tripping of a bomb from a faceless perpetrator. It made me fill with helpless anger that it was not a personal vendetta, or a nose to nose confrontation. Just a chance act of violence for reasons not associated with anything that the nine of us in that room had ever said or done.

Or, was it random? Would God allow such a reckless event for His own purposes? Was I ready to respond in a manner that would save the innocent lives of the children in my care? My life is in God's hands. I've known this for decades. He knows how and when my journey should end.

Yesterday's incident reminded me that I cannot control my life, but I can control my reactions to the circumstances that face me. My prayer is that God will guide those reactions for His own purposes in a school where seemingly capricious acts of violence are a daily possibility.

Look It Up

"And we know that all things work together for good to them that love God, to them who are the called according to his purpose."

Romans 8:28

"Thou art my hiding place; thou shalt preserve me from trouble; thou shalt compass me about with songs of deliverance."

Psalms 32:7

"When thou passest through the waters, I will be with thee; and through the rivers, they shall not overflow thee; when thou walkest through the fire; thou shalt not be burned; neither shall the flame kindle upon thee."

Isaiah 43:2

Chalk It Up

"Courage is doing what you're afraid to do. There can be no courage unless you're scared."

—Eddie Rickenbacker (Fighter pilot)

Lesson Plan

Recognize that many of the circumstances of life are out of your personal control. All that can realistically be controlled are your private reactions to those circumstances. Ask yourself: Do my students see a teacher who models mature, emotional responses that reflect a deep dependence upon God's sovereignty?

DOG EARED BOOKS

Aboy with lamb chop sideburns and bell-bottom pants smiled from the open page of the health book. In another picture, several children held signs defining the basic four food groups with long straight groovy hair. Page after page of retro-looking styles in a text over twenty years old. Frustration swept over me. "How can I teach these students with outdated material? No wonder teachers experienced problems motivating anyone to read these health books." I fumed, snapping the cover shut.

The health book represented the tip of the iceberg. The science text wore an equal number of years on its battered cover. Several outer planets have been discovered and Pluto no longer belongs to the original nine planets since the publication date, making the solar system unit obsolete. Fortunately, knowledge of plant life and botany remains steady so the vocabulary in that unit still applied. *But that's not the point. The better school districts change texts every five years so their students stay current. As much as I supplement from other sources, nothing beats a state of the art text.*

Then a letter from Africa arrived at home. My cousin, Byron Jeys, taught for two terms in the Peace Corps in Malawi, then signed on in a government run high school there. He has lived in Malawi for over twenty years, preparing the one tenth of the population who are in high school for an even more selective process to enroll in college. Ninety students in a class are not unusual. Students sit on the floor or on benches. The school furnishes a globe, map, chalk and blackboard.

In his letter, Byron wrote: "As a cost cutting measure the government has decided not to furnish books for schools. It seems like a regressive step. When I teach in Phwezi, I teach history without a book. I also taught grammar without books. For literature and comprehension, I managed to get some old books to use. Most literature teachers teach using one book."

My mind visualized my classroom, filled with novels and nonfiction books obtained through years of purchasing from bookstore bargains, parents, my own children, garage sales and book clubs. Most books were current, colorful and appealing to fourth graders. Even the classic children's books had been printed in an updated volume. In a corner of the classroom, several headsets and crates of books on tape invited students to listen to a well-presented story complete with musical background. The media center in our school boasted new editions donated by the local PTA.

Although some of the texts are sadly outdated, the district recently purchased other new curriculum. The availability of supplementary materials at my fingertips helps me bring my class into the twenty first century. Thinking of my cousin Byron, I am grateful for what is available, and am determined to teach more creatively with the resources God has given.

Look It Up

"But godliness with contentment is great gain. For we brought nothing into the world, and it is certain we can carry nothing out. And having food and rainment, let us be therewith content."

I Timothy 6:6–8

Chalk It Up

"I complained that I had no shoes until I met a man who had no feet."

–Mom Meiners

"Without regard to pay and with little thought of it, I taught anyone who wanted to learn anything that I could teach him."

–Booker T. Washington

Lesson Plan

Try teaching auditorily only with no paper/pencil. Use small chalkboards for math computation or short answers. Roll Play-dough to make letters to practice spelling words. Have students auditorily repeat information, forcing them to memorize concepts. Role play historical events.

KNOWN BY NAME

With the warmth of spring sun already heating the hall, Johnnie extended his hand to me. He stood straight, giving direct eye contact. With a smile on his lips and in his voice, Johnnie clearly enunciated, "Good morning, Mrs. Lampos."

He waited.

"Good morning, Johnnie." I returned the greeting, emphasizing Johnnie's name, wrapping it in a vocal hug. Then he moved through the door into the classroom to hang up his book bag. The next student extended her hand. Big brown eyes met mine.

"Good morning, Janessa Grace."

"Good morning, Mrs. Lampos."

Another student stepped forward and offered morning pleasantries.

After the last salutation, I reflected. We've come a long way from the first weeks of school. In the fall, my class really didn't know how to handle the morning line up. Shaking hands with dead fish would have been just as satisfying to me. Most significant, nobody made eye contact. Looking down, chin in chest, possibly a mumbled "good morning" escaped from their lips, it was hard to discern. The exchange of "mornings" reminded me of a judge handing down a death sentence to an innocent person.

For all the bravado, loud voiced comments and strutting that took place between the bus and building, this behavior puzzled me. Why so shy? So almost backward? In this neighborhood, deferring to adults is not a cultural aspect, so that did not explain the behavior. Studying their faces the next day, some students did appear genuinely bashful in the presence of an adult. Others seemed perplexed by my attempts to personalize the morning routine. Most, however, flashed fear, pulling away slightly as our hands shook, their faces turned to the side. A few actually covered their face as I said their name in greeting. A combination of low self-concept and years of physical abuse reflected in the morning line. The realization saddened me.

Slowly, day by day, perseverance chipped away at the students' defenses. "Let me see those beautiful eyes, Reem." Scared, deer like, Reem allowed a "two seconds journey to her soul" before turning her head into a down cast position.

"You're standing straight with square shoulders today, Ahmed." *But where is your face? All I see is hair.* Gently I moved Ahmed's chin up a little. Apprehension crossed his eyes. "Good morning, Ahmed," I whispered, caressing each word with my voice.

Month by month, more students genuinely returned the greeting. On one particularly cold wintry day, the buses arrived sporadically as they fought their way through drifted roads. Seatwork had already begun as the last few students plowed through the door. I kept on talking to the class as Alexis walked up to me, extended her hand, made eye contact and piped, "Good morning, Mrs. Lampos."

At that moment, I knew that the students realized the importance of the ritual. Grasping her hand, I said in a tone that I hoped would melt the snow off her boots, "Good morning, Alexis."

Look It Up

"A good name is rather to be chosen than great riches."

Proverbs 22:1

"The sheep hear his voice, and he calleth his own sheep by name."

John 10:3

"But now thus saith the Lord, that created thee, O Jacob, and he that formed thee, O Israel, Fear not: for I have redeemed thee, I have called thee by thy name, thou art mine."

Isaiah 43:1

Chalk It Up

"What is a name? Is it a conventional marker, a social construction, a mere handle? Or does it mean something in itself and either stand for some quality within the person who bears it or have the power to shape the person by acting as a sort of destiny or matrix."

–Justin Kaplan

"Things really are what they are called. Or to put it more bluntly, they are what they are because of what they are named."

–Benjamin Bleck

"As Slow grew up, he was not happy with his name. Few (Indian) boys were given names they wanted to keep. But until a child earned a new name by doing some brave or special deed, it could not be changed."

–A Boy Called Slow,
The True Story of Sitting Bull

Lesson Plan

Help children discover the origin of their name. The libraries are filled with books that give the meaning of names from African American roots to Jewish, German or Celtic beginnings. Knowing the meaning of their name could empower students to visualize themselves with the characteristics of their name.

Have the students write their own first name in block letters down the side of a piece of paper. After every letter, write verbs and adjectives that describe the student starting with that letter. Friends could help them think of appropriate values or character traits.

WHAT JOHNNY SAW

The traffic ahead of my Saturn barely crawled along the narrow street. The barred windows on the houses drove home the fact that the funeral for a student's parent was in a neighborhood riddled with fear of violence. Finally, the line of cars ahead of me stopped. Braking, I noticed the man.

He hunched over the handle of a shopping cart, slowly pushing its heaping contents along the slushy sidewalk. Caps and scarves partially hid a face weathered by the storms of a tough life. As the man moved, he talked to himself, incessantly, insistently, oblivious to the strangers in cars watching him. My heart grew heavy with sadness as he trekked through the melting snow.

"He was a little boy once. Someone loved him and cared for him. What happened?" I wondered.

The day that Johnnie Watson joined our class, I knew that there was something different about him. Tall, thin, dressed in carefully pressed shirt and pants, scrubbed face, Johnnie obviously had a parent who knew the meaning of soap and water. "It's not a sin to be poor, but it is a sin to be dirty," my own mother often quoted as I protested wearing outdated but carefully mended and pressed clothes. Johnny came from that same stock.

But it was his mannerisms that caught my attention. Johnny mumbled to himself. He talked when he walked. He spoke when he wrote. He read aloud. Sometimes his words were audible and distinguishable. Sometimes the voice was low and the words ran together. "I can't concentrate when I sit near Johnny." The complaint was issued often, so Johnny's desk traveled around the room from corner to corner trying to find an appropriate seating arrangement. Finally he sat near the door between two noise-tolerant girls who focused on their work and tuned out his monologues. Both girls lived in the small project apartments brimming with siblings and adults.

Conventional techniques in behavior management failed with Johnny. It didn't matter if he was isolated from the group, put in the hall, wrote repetitive sentences, praised when he was quiet. He always acted the same. He kept talking to himself. When I picked up the class from art, music or gym, often the teacher would be upset. "Johnny is disruptive. I sent him to the office." I understood the teacher's frustration but realized that Johnny actually look embarrassed by his actions and seemed to be trying to control a behavior that clearly controlled him.

The social worker observed him in my fourth grade class. "Could be Turret's Syndrome," she whispered over her shoulder as she dashed to the door in response to a crisis call from the intercom. "Or just emotional disturbance. Hard to tell."

Surprisingly, Johnny knew an array of trivia. "What's another name for the Big Dipper?" I asked. "'The Drinking Ground', like with Harriet Tubman leading the slaves to freedom," he shouted without raising his hand. He memorized the states and capitals before anyone else. Although comprehension proved faulty at times, Johnny decoded the fourth grade texts and achieved average and above average grades.

That's why I knew something was wrong on Monday morning. Johnny walked into the hall from the bus with his arms flapping in the air like a bird trying to take off. The other students gave him a wide berth. He mumbled under his breath in fast paced tones like a tape recorder set on the top speed. Sliding his backpack off, he took out a few items, then dashed to his desk. There he hunched over a library book, reading aloud at a furious intensity with indistinguishable words.

"Johnny. It's me. Mrs. Lampos."

His eyes moved back and forth in their sockets. He did not focus on my face.

"Is there something wrong, Johnny?"

Johnny stopped mumbling, then spoke so quickly I had to concentrate to understand his words. "I went outside. I was going to the bus. Some high school kids were there. We saw something bad." His eyes darted.

"What did you see, Johnny? Tell me."

"We seen a dead body in the empty lot. It was the lady down the block. Her arms and legs were bent funny. She had a really bad color to her skin. She was dead." He gasped for air.

"What else happened, Johnny?"

"The police came. They sent us all away. But it was time to go to the bus. That dead body was next to our back yard."

By now Johnny's legs tapped staccato beats on the tile. He rocked in his chair. Moans from deep inside him flowed through his tightly locked lips.

A tap on my shoulder drew my attention to a student with a note from the main office. "If any child comes to school with a strange story or emotional manifestations, please send them to the office."

"Johnny, take this note to the Principal. Don't come back until you've talked with her. Understand?" He nodded as I added a few sentences to the memo. Johnny flapped his arms as he left the room.

Later in the day, the faculty learned that what Johnny witnessed in his backyard was the body of the mother of eight students in our school system. A drug addict who supported her habit as a prostitute. She had given her own mother custody of her children so she could pursue her lifestyle. Her brutal murder matched those of three other drug-addicted women in the area. All of the students knew her children. Many went to the house for Halloween treats. Johnny had gotten up early in the morning with the high schoolers and saw the body.

That week, Johnny experienced problems focusing on his work. His monologue increased in volume and intensity. I called his mother. She reported that he screamed through nightmares and refused to go outside to play. She said the yellow tape from the police and investigators made the lot unusable as the block's baseball field. The kids had no place to play.

I often think of Johnny, especially when encountering men pushing loaded carts, talking to themselves, off in their own worlds. Once they sat as students in a classroom. They participated as part of a family. Hopefully, they were valued. Maybe, like Johnny, these men were exposed to a violent world at a young age. They saw too much too soon and could not process the information.

God places each child in my class for a reason. Most of the time, that purpose is so I can learn to reach out with compassion to a child who needs that extra bit of love and understanding. This year, that child was Johnny.

Look It Up

"Do ye look on things after the outward appearance?"

II Corinthians 10:7

"For the Lord seeth not as man seeth, for man looketh on the outward appearance, but the Lord looketh on the heart."

Samuel 16:7

Chalk It Up

"Affection and love mean expressing appreciation for the very being of a child, for those characteristics and abilities that are part of the total package of the person."

–Gary Chapman

"The measure of any person is how he treats those who are less gifted, less intelligent, and less able. The measure of a Christian is how willing he or she is to reach down and help those who are less fortunate."

–Frank Peretti

"We don't ask a flower to give us any special reasons for its existence. We look at it and we are able to accept it as being something different, and different from ourselves."

–Gwendolyn Brooks

Lesson Plan

Read a book that focuses on new ways to relate to your students. Try *The Five Love Languages of Children*, by Gary Chapman; *Hide and Seek*, by James Dobson; or *Every Child Can Succeed*, by Cynthia Ulrich Tobias. Those, or other books, help a teacher to understand the heart of a child, not their outward appearance.

THE SIGN OF THE STAR

Snowflakes drifted in the sky. A cold wind from the north whistled against the bricks of our classroom. My six behavior disordered fifth grade boys and I enjoyed the cozy warmth of our office size classroom. We were making Christmas cards for the local nursing home as part of an all-school project.

"You can make a cutout of any traditional Christmas symbol for the cover of your card. What would we use? That's right, Darius, a bell like the Salvation Army rings outside the grocery store. A wreath. Good, Juan." Both items easily emerged in chalky sketches. "How about a star?" I suggested, turning to the board and quickly executing a five pointed star.

Total silence from the students behind me. Then frantic whispers.

"Erase that, Mrs. Lampos."

"You sure be in big trouble if the principal sees that."

"Gang signs are illegal in school, Mrs. Lampos. Everyone knows that."

Immediately the offending star disappeared from the blackboard.

"There's another way to make a star." I stated, turning once more to the board.

With geometric precision, two equilateral triangles produced a six sided star. "This is the Star of David. You've probably seen it on the flag of Israel during the Olympics." Stepping aside, I let them view my newest offering. The class gasped in unison.

"I've only seen that star sprayed on the sides of buildings by taggers." said Darius.

"Erase that one really quick."

"Why?" I asked innocently.

"It's a sign of our rival gang," Juan instructed.

"You's gonna get us all suspended, Mrs. Lampos. I can't get in no more trouble with my Grandma, so erase that." Calvin pointed to the six sided star on the board.

As I erased this star, my heart broke. The star of Bethlehem that shone over the manger, signaling hope to mankind had been twisted into a symbol of violence. In the neighborhood in which these boys fought to survive, the beauty of the star had been transferred into the ugliness of bloodshed. The star was a gang sign.

Reaching back into a half century of Christmas cards, I remembered another version of the nativity star. Turning to the board, I chalked a four-sided elongated star, adding beams of light from the sides. Lifting my eyebrows, I waited for comments.

"That star's okay," said Darius.

"No gang around here has that kind of sign," added Juan.

"Okay. A star can be a Christmas symbol that our older citizens will recognize. There is construction paper and glitter on the back table. Choose something you can make and do a good job."

As the boys began cutting and pasting, I walked among their desks, silently praying, "Lord, in their drug infested, bullet riddled existence, let my students find the Prince of Peace. Let the Star of Bethlehem illuminate their lives with Truth. Help them to learn the Christmas message."

Hearing my footsteps, Darius lifted his head from his work. He smiled radiantly towards me as he held up his construction paper card. A yellow four-sided star shone from excessive glitter against a midnight blue background. Underneath, in white pencil, Darius had written "Merry Christmas."

Look It Up

"There came wise men from the east to Jerusalem saying, 'Where is he that is born King of the Jews? for we have seen his star in the east and are come to worship him.' When they saw the star, they rejoiced with exceeding great joy."

Matthew 2:1–2, 10

"The people that walked in darkness have seen a great light; they that dwell in the shadow of death, upon them hath the light shined."

Isaiah 9:2

Chalk It Up

"Suddenly I was asking myself: 'Suppose you were to be granted a wish for these kids. What would be the one best thing you could hope for?' And I knew my answer: that they could begin life all over again, with the fresh and innocent personalities of newborn children. And more: that this time as they were growing up they could be surrounded by love instead of by hate and fear. . . . But it would take a miracle. A series of miracles such as I've never seen."

–David Wilkerson,
founder of Teen Challenge

Lesson Plan

Get into the minds of your students. Symbols that mean one thing to our generation, to our socio-economic group or to our circle of friends may have an entirely different meaning in the world of our children. Words often denote other connotations that we ascribe to them. Communication depends on accurately conveying ideas and emotions. Become a part of your students' vocabulary, symbols and signs so your voice speaks accurately.

SLEEPLESS NIGHTS AND SECURE DAYS

The other students were taking off their winter coats and unloading their backpacks when Brandon slouched through the doorway. He paused inside the classroom, head down, shoulders drooping. I went over to shake his hand with the "good morning" greeting, but never got the chance.

"Mrs. Lampos." Brandon turned his head up to me. His eyes squinted tightly against the bright morning sunlight streaming in the window. Deep furrows dug into his forehead. "I don't feel well. My head hurts. My stomach aches." His arms hugged his midsection.

Stooping to his level told more of the story. Brandon's face was an ashen color. He slumped against the wall.

"My mom and her boyfriend fought all night. I had to protect my mom. I didn't get any sleep. I feel terrible."

What a way to start the day, I reflected.

Putting my hand on his shoulder, I guided him to the coat rack. "Put your head down on your desk until you feel better."

Brandon hung up his coat, and by the time that the attendance and lunch money envelope had been filled in, he slept soundly with his head cradled in his arms.

Forty minutes later, I woke Brandon.

"We're going to the computer lab. You can't stay alone in the room."

The short nap left Brandon groggy. He stood in line with a comatose expression. His feet barely shuffled on the tile. This kid needed to sleep!

Now, two choices confronted me. One, let Brandon lay on the carpeting on the opposite side of the computer lab, possibly on a coat. Two, take him to the nurse's office and let him sleep on the little bed in there. The latter choice seemed most logical, but froth with difficulty. Mainly, getting past the secretary.

The class lined up in the hall. I ushered Brandon into the office.

"Mrs. Jones. This child has a headache. He needs to sleep in the nurse's room."

"Does he have a fever?"

"No, he has a headache and upset stomach."

"Call home and get his mother to come get him."

Irritation set my teeth scraping. Brandon's mother doesn't need the school calling her I angrily thought. She has all she can do to survive the day herself.

"His mother is at work." I paused, then leaned across the desk. My steely gaze locked onto the secretary's eyes. "This child needs to sleep."

Miss Jones pulled back in her padded chair. Annoyance creased her face. "Okay. Just for a while."

Brandon flopped onto the vinyl bed, assumed a fetal position, then closed his eyes immediately. Pausing for a moment, I allowed a flood of memories to pass through my mind. Deeply repressed images of my sister and me. Up all night. Defending our mother from the blows of our drunken stepfather. Hiding the domestic violence the next day at school with overachievement. Pushing down the pain. Pretending everything was all right.

How I longed for sleep on some of those days. Perhaps even for compassion. But keeping the family secret meant playing a part. Even as a child, it was necessary to paste on a smile and overachieve so everything would seem normal from the outside. Looking at Brandon, I was thankful that he could talk to me. To tell me what he needed. So that he could get some rest in the safety of school.

Look It Up

"I was hungry and you gave me something to eat, I was thirsty and you gave me something to drink, I was a stranger and you invited me in, I needed clothes and you clothed me, I was sick and you came to visit me."

Matthew 25:35–36

"You have been a refuge for the poor, a refuge for the needy in his distress, a shelter from the storm and a shade from the heat."

Isaiah 25:4

Chalk It Up

"There are two important times in the lives of school-age children: to be touched emotionally by their parents on leaving and returning home gives them security and courage to face the challenges of the day."

–Gary Chapman and Ross Campbell

Lesson Plan

The student who is quiet may be too quiet. Disappearing into the woodwork may be a strategy for hiding pain. Take time to talk to the child who hides behind a wall of silence. Get to know their heart and needs. Given time, they may share their deepest concerns and desires. For once, the squeaky wheel should be left ungreased.

A CUP OF COLD WATER

Sunlight reflected off the snow blinding my eyes. I leaned to the left so the brick wall blocked the glare. It also blocked the view of incoming car rider students, which was the reason for standing in this spot anyway. Shielding my eyes with my hand made tracking these bundled children easier.

Nicole's noisy nose signaled her presence. The sniffling sounds created when she cried and didn't have a handkerchief. The third grade teacher, Mrs. Barrette, her arm on Nicole's back shoulders, ambled down the hall in my direction. Nicole shuffled her feet, sobbing with muffled cries. Her head sank into her coat like a trapped turtle hiding in its hard shell.

"She got on the bus this morning really hysterical. Crying uncontrollably. The bus driver asked what was wrong." Mrs. Barrette spoke directly in my ear as a matter of confidentiality. "Nicole's mother yelled at her before the bus came. Been a bad morning."

Mrs. Barrette tightened her lips, turned, and dashed back to her class which was quickly lined up at the far end of the hallway.

I stooped down. "Can you talk about it, Nicole?" With a light touch of my fingers on her chin, Nicole raised her head. Hurt and rejection rolled with hot tears down her cheeks.

"Mommy came home about two this morning from her job. She's a cocktail waitress, you know." Nicole paused to inhale mucus and heave her thin shoulders. In my mind, I visualized Nicole's mother at the teacher's conference. Very young, but with a face hardened by the trials of life. Several tattoos decorated her wrists and arms. Her voice had snapped out words as her leg tapped nervously. Not a picture of patience. Maybe the product of poor parenting herself.

Nicole continued between gasps of breath. "Mommy was tired. Daddy made her get up and get me and my sister ready for school. She screamed at us and said she hated us. She never wanted us to be born."

Nicole started to cry all over again. A spray from fresh tears splashed onto my cheeks. Instinctively, my hand wiped the mist away. Reaching my arms around her little body, I held Nicole close to my heart.

With the practiced hug of a grandmother of six, compassion and care flowed from me to Nicole. "I'm glad you're here at school with us. We want you here. You are a very special child, Nicole."

Holding her at arm's length, I looked deep into her eyes for a moment. "Let's go have a good day together, Nicole. Okay?"

After a brief pause and a few more waterworks, she responded. "Okay." A tiny glint of a smile graced Nicole's lips as she hauled the backpack onto her shoulders.

As we strolled slowly toward the hallway to our noisily waiting classroom, I remembered a thin straggly haired blond girl soaking her neck scarves with tears as she trudged to school. Her stepfather had cursed her again. The sound of his rejection rang in her head for years.

Look It Up

"And whosoever shall give drink unto one of these little ones a cup of cold water only in the name of a disciple.....he shall in no wise lose his reward."

Matthew 10:42

Chalk It Up

"If your last encounter in the morning and your first encounter in the evening is to speak the primary love language of your children, you will be performing one of the most meaningful deeds of the day. And, this just might have a positive impact on their motivation for learning.

—Gary Chapman and Ross Campbell

"I is kind. I is smart. I is important."

—Mae Mobley, The Help

Lesson Plan

Marva Collins advises her parents of Westside Preparatory School in Chicago that "When you send your children off to school in the morning, boost their self-images with encouraging words." Many of our students have been sent off with a deluge of cursing and negativity. Our task is to reverse that defeated self-image before the day begins so that some learning can take place. We will never know how much our kind words in the morning healed open wounds.

AND TO ALL A GOOD NIGHT

As Thanksgiving and Christmas approach, my stomach begins to knot in a familiar, nauseating way. Waves of depression wash me, drowning happy thoughts and transporting them into a sea of sorrow. Although time has mellowed these feelings, every year I struggle to have an outward show of holiday cheer.

Maybe that's why the sounds of sleigh bells compel me to read *I Wish My Daddy Didn't Drink So Much*, by Judith Vigna. It's not the kind of cheery, festive story that one expects a teacher to read during a time of mistletoe and merriment. Realistically written, the plot depicts a young girl's holiday of broken promises from her father who throws the holiday turkey across the room and scares her into hiding behind the couch. The hope of the story lies in the compassion of a neighbor lady who knows the family from Alcoholics Anonymous. Hardly typical Christmas literature. Unfortunately, a book that relates with many of the students in my class.

Kevin responded to the story. "My parents always get drunk

on Christmas Eve. They invite their friends over and everyone drinks a lot. Us kids finish up their leftovers. I had a hard time walking up the stairs to my bedroom." Kevin rolled his head and eyes.

"My dad drinks from Thanksgiving to New Year's Day," inserted Jessica. "We just stay out of his way because he gets real mean when he's drunk." She hunched into her sweatshirt like a turtle.

"Last year my grandma came over on Christmas. She said mommy had the flu again. We made the turkey and Stove-top dressing together. That was fun."

"Uncle Bill gets drunk every Christmas Eve and yells at my dad. They even get in a fight sometimes. Once they smashed the ping pong table."

"Everyone gives me a sip from their drinks. I like the way it feels. Grandpa says kids should enjoy some Christmas cheer, too."

Laurie sat balanced on her chair with her arms wrapped around her knees. "I don't like the whole holiday thing. My mommy cries a lot. We don't have a lot of money because mommy's boyfriend is at the bar most of the time. When he comes back to the apartment, he yells and gets mean."

I read the book near the end of the school day so the ticking of the clock stops the onslaught of information that bursts from the class like confetti from a holiday cracker. So why do I keep reading the book?

From experience, I know that there is a child in my class who works every day to do their best because high grades mean life is normal. A child who fights to stay awake after a sleepless night of brawling adults. A child who worries if mom will be physically safe during the day, or if there will be a home to go to after school. If they will be in protective custody again. If the police will knock on their door. If long sleeves will cover bruises on the arms.

I read the story so one student in my care won't feel alone in their private holiday nightmare. Maybe this child can look at me, know my story, and see hope. With the knowledge that one child is being helped, maybe the dark clouds won't gather as thickly for me this holiday season. The memories won't be so vivid. And the pain will slip away.

Look It Up

"They that sow in tears shall reap in joy"

Psalms 126:5

"God of all comfort who comforts us in all our affliction so that we may be able to comfort those who are in any affliction with the comfort with which we ourselves are comforted by God."

II Corinthians 1:3–4

Chalk It Up

"God does not waste an ounce of our pain or a drop of our tears; suffering doesn't come our way for no reason, and He seems especially efficient at using what we endure to mold our character."

–Frank Peretti

"God grant me the serenity to accept the things I cannot change, courage to change the things I can, and the wisdom to know the difference."

–Serenity Prayer from AA

"Step One-We admitted we were powerless over alcohol—that our lives had become unmanageable.
Step Two–We came to believe that a Power greater than ourselves could restore us to sanity."

Twelve Steps from Alcoholic Anonymous

Lesson Plan

As the adult child of an alcoholic, my life carries emotional scars and open wounds that need to heal. Secrecy is one of the alcoholic family's worst strategies for coping. By sharing my experience of growing up with an alcoholic stepfather, my students can know that they are not alone. Most important, they believe that it is possible to survive and thrive. That provides hope and the ability to live life, one day at a time.

FROM DIFFERENT EYES

Reem's brown eyes searched my face, then rested on my baby blues. For a long moment, our souls communed, and then she turned her gaze downward. A cultural gesture that had become familiar. There had been a pleading in Reem's eyes that puzzled me. But, since 9–11 shatttered our world two weeks ago, nothing really made sense anymore.

"Well, Reem are you back to visit the old room for Open House?" I nodded toward the classroom half filled with parents and students milling around desks and viewing artwork on the walls.

"I came to see you." The earnestness in Reem's voice focused my attention. "I am not in this school this year. My parents transferred me to the Muslim School in the next suburb. My little sister still goes to this school. My parents are visiting her room."

Reem's parents emigrated from Palestine to America several years earlier. With thick accents and tough determination, the family created a moderate lifestyle in a land of opportunity. Their emphasis on Reem's education impressed me.

"Has it been difficult for you to go to school?" I asked, knowing the answer.

Staring at the floor, she replied. "Everyday when I go to school, I am afraid. There are angry Americans everywhere and I don't know what will happen."

The day after the Twin Towers collapsed, the youth in my suburb responded by driving up and down the main streets with large American flags draped on their hoods or flying from car windows. They congregated on one particular street corner, their size swelling to over three hundred. Chanting, the crowd marched to the next suburb, waving their flags, as a show of patriotism. Their destination: the Muslim mosque and school.

For five days, the mob's size rose and fell like the tide, but the chants never stopped. From the spirited "U.S.A.," eventually came "Burn the mosque." As a SWAT team stood guard, police and firemen from several communities formed a thin blue line of protection around the school and mosque. This military contingency constituted Reem's morning reception as her parents took her to classes, and the words that rang in her ears as they drove her home in the afternoon.

I waited for Reen's eyes to fix on mine. "My son-in-law is one of those firemen standing guard over you. I know he would never let anyone harm children. There are people there who want to protect you. Trust them. Reem, I'm sorry that this is happening to you." She seemed to understand.

Innocent people. Caught in the quagmire of racial profiling and revenge. My heart broke because the cycle of prejudice continued so relentlessly.

Look It Up

"And whoever welcomes a little child like this in my name welcomes me."

Matthew 18:5

"Accept one another, then, just as Christ accepted you, in order to bring praise to God."

Romans 15:7

Chalk It Up

"We are common earthenware jars, filled with the treasure of the riches of God. The jar is not important-the treasure is everything."

–Corrie ten Boom

"I like the idea of us all being here."

–Gwendolyn Brooks

Lesson Plan

Children in a society built on diversity gain a wealth of knowledge and understanding from meeting so many people from varying backgrounds. Embedded in that same opportunity is the insidiousness of prejudice. As teachers, we should be sensitive to the children in our care and ensure their safety from those who cannot see beyond stereotypes. "Lord, make me an instrument of your peace."

HIDDEN TREASURE

My husband, Vern put his arm around me as we sat in the half-filled chapel on a hot July, Sunday evening. Our decision to come and support our church's teenage volunteers for work camp was the right one. Fixing up poverty housing in West Virginia beckoned like a vacation to them, but reality would set in when the work started.

The volunteers filed in and beamed at the audience from the front of the church. Scanning the row of muscular fellows and bubbly girls, my eyes suddenly dipped. About half the height of the young men on either side of him, Joey nonetheless squared off to gain every vertical inch possible. My heart beat in awe just seeing him there.

Vern and I knew Joey from our years working in Children's Church. Joey started attending at age seven. He challenged every management skill Vern and I had acquired. Joey crawled under chairs. He blasted loud noises. He sauntered around the room. His speech bordered on unintelligible. We tried to incorporate him into the service, but it was tough.

That's when Joey's adoptive mother, Kathy Taylor, introduced herself and supplied needed background on Joey. As a teacher in the language disordered classroom of a large metropolitan school, Miss Taylor taught many students from foster homes. Joey touched her heart from the first time he set foot in her room. As she worked on speech remediation, Kathy suspected a bright child hopelessly trapped in a body that could not communicate. Although expressive language lagged, Joey's intelligence level soared. Fetal alcohol syndrome left Joey with a potpourri of abilities. As a single person, Kathy Taylor decided to adopt Joey.

The next year proved grueling ones for both Kathy and Joey. Visits to specialists for accurate assessments. Joey's strengths and weaknesses drained both of them: swimming lessons to strengthen gross motor skills, karate lessons, church activities, extra tutoring and other educational experiences filled the weekends and after school hours. But time and opportunities chiseled away at the rough corners and Joey took on some polished edges. By the time high school rolled around, Joey survived in a mainstreamed program.

Kathy Taylor, and the uncounted adoptive teachers that she represents, demonstrates the capacity to glimpse beyond the surface problems of a child to their potential. When social workers, foster care or children's church leaders encountered Joey, all his exasperating traits held them at bay. Kathy reached beyond the rough exterior and grasped Joey's possibilities as someone who cared. Then she took him into her home and her heart so Joey's life could change.

Glancing over my shoulder in the chapel, I spotted Kathy in another pew. She sat with her recently adopted teenage daughter. A proud smile graced Kathy's lips as she gazed at Joey in the front of the church. Her diamond in the tough.

Look It Up

"By this all men will know that you are my disciples, if you love one another."

John 13:35

"But we have this treasure in earthen vessels."

II Corinthians 4:7

"For the Lord seeth not as man seeth; for man looketh on the outward appearance, but the Lord looketh on the heart."

I Samuel 16:7

Chalk It

"Adoption has reaffirmed some of life's important lessons: parenting is a privilege. It is our work and joy to honor that commitment. Love and trust are enormous gifts we give to one another in life. Treasure every moment with your child, enjoy the adventure.

–Fran Durbin,
adoptive parent and teacher

Lesson Plan

So many times as teachers we let the annoying habits and behaviors of a child blind us to the potential that lies deep within. Sometimes it becomes difficult to find the positive aspects of a student. By tapping into those strengths, we could possibly change the course of that child's life.

MALCOLM'S STORY

Pushing frustration aside, I restated my position in a voice much calmer than the feelings racing through my mind.

"As much as I would like to work with Malcolm, a regular education classroom is not equipped to meet the needs of an emotionally disturbed child. Besides, the year is three quarters gone. He will be new to any class he goes into." The logic appeared clear to me.

The social worker leaned into the tabletop area. "You won't be alone in dealing with Malcolm's behavior, Mrs. Lampos. He will be scheduled for two twenty minute sessions per week with me."

That is, if you don't have a conference, a meeting or illness. I've been down that road a few times.

"Malcolm will come to me for twenty minutes at the end of each day." The special education resource teacher beamed from across the table. "That should help."

"With this wonderful teamwork, Malcolm has no choice but to turn around his behavior. All Malcolm requires is a fresh start. That's why his parents sent him to live with us. A new environment." Malcolm's uncle settled the matter right then and there.

The principal breathed with relief as the director of special services finished the paperwork. Malcolm was mine.

Teaching emotionally disturbed and behavior disordered students in a self-contained classroom for eight years drained, stressed and challenged me. Daily adrenaline rushes sustained me during those conflicts with students. This recent assignment to regular education brought sanity.

Knowledge can be a dangerous thing, and full knowledge of Malcolm's behavioral potential frightened and enraged me. The paperwork from out of state confirmed my worst fears. "Needs an alternative school placement. Anger control issues must be addressed. Threat to other students and adults. Hair trigger temper. Explosive." No academic goals for this brighter than average ten year old. Only behavior. To such an emotionally disturbed child, a regular classroom is like a ravenous wolf to a flock of sheep. Anger at the injustice of the situation engulfed me. In better moments, my heart cried out to God for wisdom.

Behaviors burst from Malcolm starting day one. He slumped in his seat. He laid his head on the desktop. Moans and groans greeted assignments. Books slammed onto the floor. Malcolm teased girls and bullied boys. With each incident, my blood pressure soared as my voice tensed. Desperately trying to stay calm on the outside, a head of steam built within me. Any hair-trigger threatened to ignite it.

"A soft answer turns away wrath." The concept kept bouncing in my head like a ball strung to a paddle board. As snappy phrases or put downs sparked on the edge of my tongue, "a soft answer turns away wrath" stopped me from speaking. After long pauses of silent fighting with clenched jaws for verbal control, teacher-like instructions replaced the malicious words.

"Make a good choice, Malcolm. You know the right way to act." Strangely, Malcolm chose the appropriate behavior as I chose to speak civilly, not from anger.

Soon, my comments moved to compliments as I "caught him being good." Malcolm recognized that positive behavior brought approval and caught my eye before trying out an appropriate action; I tried to reinforce that behavior with a confirming comment.

The social worker set up a behavior chart that went home each day. Malcolm received consequences from his uncle so the report carried weight with him. Malcolm zeroed in on the five chosen behaviors and started to modify them. Together we ranked his behavior from one to five at the end of the day before he went to the resource room. That five minutes provided a special time for us to talk.

The weeks flew by as Malcolm experienced lapses in behavior. He left the dismissal line and was lost in the building after school. He verbally fought and alienated other students. One day he brought a cigarette lighter to school with the threat to burn the building down. That cost him two days of suspension.

Then Mother's Day rolled onto the calendar. Like many others in the classroom, Malcolm lived with relatives and making Mother's Day cards constituted a touchy subject. The rather liberal definition of mother fit our students' context. Malcolm's mother had died, and his dad remarried. Serious issues between Malcolm and his stepmother precipitated. That is why his request surprised me.

"Mrs. Lampos. I know I live with Auntie Luella, but can I make a card for my stepmother, too?"

"Sure can. She's your mother now, just like your Aunt Luella is."

Malcolm's fingers flew as he cut, trimmed and glued heart doilies onto a card. Taking a piece of notebook paper, he wrote a note.

"Dear Mom,

I know that you and me have had a lot of trouble getting along. I know that I have not done everything right. If I get a chance to come home, I will act different.

Your stepson, Malcolm."

Malcolm showed me the card. "Can you mail it?" Malcolm knew his parent's address. I mailed his card and letter. Several weeks later, his dad and stepmother drove from out of state to our school to pick up his report card. They took him home for the summer with the hope of registering him in a private school for the next year. They walked out the door as a family.

In my mind echoed the advice, "A soft answer turns away wrath."

Look It Up

"A soft answer turns away wrath, but grievous words stir up anger."

Proverbs 15:1

"A word fitly spoken is like apples of gold in pictures of silver."

Proverbs 25:11

Chalk It Up

"When the pain becomes great enough, a child will do almost anything to make tomorrow different than today."

–L. Tobin

"Behind every act of misbehavior lies a strength-a desire to express needs and not give in. Children with less spirit give up, withdraw or maybe just conform. You have to admire the vitality of spirit in children who are willing to fight."

–L. Tobin

Lesson Plan

We all respond well to compliments that are sincere and specific. An angry child is no exception. Looking for the good in a disruptive student takes self-control and effort, but the reward is a positive attitude. So, take one more concentrated evaluation of a problem child. Find a quality worth praising. Then present the praise in a timely manner. If nothing else, you'll throw the student off guard.

TO THE OTHER MOTHER

Rocking the toddler in her arms, trying to get her to sleep, Mrs. Carpenter noticed a smoky smell. "Someone's burning trash again," she thought. "Can't see a thing out this upstairs window." Getting two babies down for a nap engrossed her attention, so she didn't notice the flames licking the bottom window, she shoved the rickety sash high and yelled for help. Two teenage boys raced to the open window and caught the two toddlers as she carefully dropped them. Then the teens helped her escape the second floor death trap as firemen hosed the kitchen area of the house. That had been a month ago.

Now, glancing about the sparsely furnished living room of the Carpenter's temporary housing, I saw sparkling clean floors and dust free end tables. They spoke volumes. While talking to Mrs. Carpenter, children of various ages walked mutely through the room, giving me a once over. Only Darius, my fourth grade student and his little two-year-old sister, held in Mrs. Carpenter's arms, remained.

The teacher who accompanied me, Mrs. Humpf, spoke. "On behalf of the staff of our school, we want to present you with this gift." Mrs. Humpf held out an envelope of money.

Mrs. Carpenter will need every penny of that, I thought as Mrs. Humpf released the envelope. Eleven children to feed and clothe. How does she do it?

Like so many grandparents, the Carpenters stepped in to rescue their eight grandchildren from the foster care system after their daughter fell victim to violent crime in the drug infested streets of their community. Darius and his two siblings joined the family during the summer when Mrs. Carpenter's niece became entangled in the court system. Eleven children from ages two to sixteen. Yet the house gleamed with cleanliness. Its walls held peace and calmness.

Mrs. Carpenter's face glowed with love and patience. "Thank you. Ever since the fire burned most of our house, we've had to make do here." Her hand gestured to the small living room. "Repairs on the house will be done by summer. We'll be moving back then."

A strong religious belief. A tremendous capacity to love. The ability to cope with adversity. At their midlife, Mr. and Mrs. Carpenter have chosen to raise eleven motherless children. They join the uncounted senior citizens who extraordinarily contribute and sacrifice for the next generation as foster parents.

In our family, my Aunt Lois served as our unofficial foster care system. At one time or another, Aunt Lois took care of most of my cousins for varying lengths of time and for differing reasons. Her frame house in mid-Iowa became a refuge for my sister and me for over a year as my mother battled with an alcoholic husband in another state. Aunt Lois provided stability and protection at a time when my sister and I displayed emotional signs from abuse. She infused us with hope because we had lost ours. Aunt Lois became "our other mother."

To women like Mrs. Carpenter and Aunt Lois, a lot of adults owe debts of gratitude that can never be paid. The "other mother" saved our lives.

Look It Up

"But the midwives feared God, and....saved the men children alive."

Exodus 1:17

"God blessed these women who protected life....They were mothers who stood in the middle between God and the birth mother to protect a life."

–Debbie Salter Goodwin

Chalk It Up

"Many times it is the other mother in the lives of our children who make an important difference. Other mothers may be more objective and do not fear rejection. Other mothers do not replace any mother in the life of a child. They simply act as midwives on a mission to save a child from disaster . . . There should never be a motherless child. God calls other mothers to fill such empty places."

–Debbie Salter Goodwin

"We all can listen and hear the call of God to befriend, mentor and love the children we cross paths with—to allow our lives to become the bridge that provides a safe crossing for a child."

–Jody Moreen, editor, *Adoption Blessings*

Lesson Plan

Search for the "other mothers" on your class list. These women are parenting under difficult conditions. Offer support and resources to encourage them. Listen to their concerns and share their burdens.

The Other Mother

In remembrance and respect for Lois Thompson, my "other mother"–Maralyn Dettmann

The sun

slid . . .

slid away . . .

Shrieking red rays

reached for the child,

yet crawling among the rocks

that broke a rising tide.

As that tide rose,

echoes of

"my child!!!" . . . in crimson,

"my child!!!" . . . in orange,

"my child!!!" . . . in deep purple . . .

and then the

Immeasurable Shadow
oversaw the whimpers.
At first,
almost unnoticed,
the moon crept
to perch overhead
—a quiet lamp
haloed with stars.
All through the night
she watched the babe
and forestalled the tide,
melting it to a lullabye;
her beams falling
o'er the tiny restless form,
until soft birds throats
opened, one by one.
The distant call . . .
"my child" . . . in faint silver . . .
"my child" . . . a faded yellow . . .
"my child!" . . . a creeping gold . . .
The arm/beams reached,
sparking echoed rainbows
on the clouds.
Smiling quietly,
the moon crept
away with the shadows.

THE UNTOUCHABLE

"Will you feed me?"

Those were John's first words one morning as my aide, Mrs. Sanchez, opened the classroom door. He was tardy again.

"Certainly. You look hungry," I heard her answer. "Do graham crackers and milk sound good?"

John grinned broadly while taking his seat in my class for boys, aged 9 to 12, with emotional or behavioral disorders. Mrs. Sanchez walked toward the door to get the milk. She peered at me over her shoulder as her expressive face asked, *What's next?*

From the first January day that John appeared at school, I was not surprised he was diagnosed as emotionally disturbed. His shell-shocked expression, coupled with a strange smile on his lips, could have scared off older kids. The scars on his face told their own stories. The pervasive odor of stale urine followed him.

John lasted half a morning in a regular fifth-grade class before having an altercation with the young, male teacher, who unceremoniously brought him to the principal's office.

Waiting for his Individual Educational Plan to arrive so he could be assigned to a special-education class, John sat in the secretary's busy room two days in a row. Agitation and boredom finally erupted in an argument with the principal. John shouted angrily in the office and ran down the school's long corridor to hide. The principal called the police.

Minutes later, my class watched out the window as police handcuffed John and placed him in a nearby squad car. The boy in cuffs was just a skinny, underclothed kid from the ghetto desperately trying to attend school. Standing near the glass panes, I fought back tears.

The next day, John was officially placed in my classroom. "Do the best you can, Cleo," the head of special education advised, "Nobody expects miracles."

Inevitably, the day arrived when John defied the rules. Like most classrooms, we observed the principle that nobody could speak rudely or intimidate another member in the class.

"Hey, nerd." From across the room, I heard John's angry, coarse whisper addressing the boy seated next to him. "I'm going to beat you up after school."

John pounded his clenched fist into his open palm, emphasizing his threat with tightened eyes and a sneer. The intended victim glared back, reading to fight on the spot.

I hurried over to John and calmly asked, "I heard what you said. You know our rules. Ten minutes in Time Out to think about what you are doing. We'll talk when you have cooled down."

John glanced around the room, refusing to budge.

"Either go voluntarily, or I'll help you." This was no idle threat.

"Don't touch me. I'll kill anyone who touches me. I'll go."

Stomping his feet as he headed to Time Out, John punctuated his last steps with "Nobody—ever—touches—me." Walking past the cabinet setting off a private space in the back of the room, John kicked and pounded the wall.

The dull thuds of shoes beating concrete died away slowly. Five minutes later, I went to the Time Out area. Taller than myself, John had crumpled his body into the fetal position, completely filling the space under the desk. I heard soft, slurpy sounds as John sucked his thumb, eyes closed, body rocking in tiny motions. The boy acted tough, but he was a frightened, fragile child inside.

John's behavior that day should have warned me for what happened several weeks later on the playground. Mrs. Sanchez usually kept a close eye on him, but one day a screaming girl drew her attention away from John. As he raced by another playground aide in what she felt was an uncontrolled manner, the woman grabbed him by the sweatshirt.

"Don't touch me!" He screamed. "Nobody touches me!"

Clutching the aide by the shoulders, John shook her with all the force he could muster. Dashing to her rescue, Mrs. Sanchez pried John's hands from the terrified woman. Street survival instincts had overridden any social skills we had taught John.

Because of the incident, John and I spent two weeks of lunchtime together. Alone with me in the room, John no longer acted with macho bravado. He was safe from the confusion of playground noise and activity.

While building intricate Lego creations, John would talk. I discovered he had survived a neighborhood of gangs, drugs and deprivation. He had lived part of one winter in a house with no heat or running water.

Soon the weather dropped to arctic conditions. Strong winds whipped across icy snowbanks.

On such a morning, after the buses had rolled in, the only missing class member was John. Mrs. Sanchez filled out the absence report so the school could call home to check on him. His mother answered the phone with the voice of someone awakened from a sound sleep.

"We overslept again." she yawned.

About an hour after school had begun, I noticed movement on the frozen front lawn. A long figure trudged through banks of snow, head lowered into the wind. The class spotted John at the same time. With noses pressed against the frigid window, we watched him make his way to the side entrance. Mrs. Sanchez opened the door for this child who had walked over two miles to come to school.

Later in the year, the youngster came to school one morning acting agitated. His body twitched nervously. When he laid his head on the desktop and fell asleep, nobody bothered him. John dozed for an hour.

Then as I read with a student, movement across the room caught my eye. John was lying on his chair, parallel to the floor, quivering violently.

"He's having a seizure." I told Mrs. Sanchez while running to the flailing child. Within seconds she had cleared the other boys form the room and called the nurse from a nearby school.

I laid John on his side so fluid could drain from his mouth. Placing his sweatshirt under his head, I held him as steady as possible while his body convulsed and lost continence.

Within five minutes, the nurse knelt beside me. Ten minutes later, the ambulance arrived. Despite no reports of seizures in John's health records, I chided myself for missing the warning signs.

Just before school one spring morning, several members of our faculty met for an informal prayer meeting. Mrs. Smith, the fourth-grade teacher, was to face the murderer of her only son. The trial of the man who had brutally killed her college-age child promised to be emotionally draining for her. Tears flowed freely as the staff held hands in a circle around her. One by one, each of us prayed for justice. Finally, the harshly ringing bell signaled the start of a new school day.

In this emotional state, I walked outside to welcome the students as they unloaded noisily from the buses. Every time I wiped away tears, fresh ones fell unchecked.

Through a watery haze, I watched John emerge from the bus with his usual cocky attitude. Clamping my lips together, I forced a quivery smile in his direction.

"What's wrong?" I heard John whisper loudly to a nearby boy.

The other student gave a hasty explanation for the weepy faculty. "Mrs. Smith's kid was killed." he began.

John stared hard in my direction. His face softened. Slowly, he stepped toward me. With a tenderness I had never seen him show, the boy wrapped his arms around me in a sympathetic hug.

"I'm touching you." I informed him softly, tears streaming.

"It's okay. Just this once." John grinned.

I learned a valuable lesson that morning. As a teacher, it had been so easy to judge John by outward appearance and ignore his inner struggles. Because he was familiar with hurt, John alone reached out in empathy to comfort me. Beyond the scars, the darting eyes, the actions and reactions, was a child made sensitive by the continual pain of his own life. With that hug, John touched my heart and I touched his.

John's struggles continued. His mother was arrested and released for alleged drug possession during the weekend before summer vacation. The next day, fire blazed through the apartment building where his family lived. John joined the ranks of the homeless yet again. Fortunately, his great-grandfather took the children and their mother into his own small house until they moved out of the district several weeks later.

Our faculty gathered various sizes of clothing and boxes of food for the household. Even in light of the tragedy John faced, a few teachers commented, "I'm giving, but I'll bet his mother sells these things for drugs."

As my students carried the donations to the trunk of John's great-grandfather's car, the preteen's haunting words echoed in my mind.

"Will you feed me?"

Then I realized—John had fed me.

Look It Up

"Carry each other's burdens, and in this way you will fulfill the law of Christ."

Galatians 6:2

"You have been a refuge for the poor, a refuge for the needy in his distress, a shelter from the storm and a shade from the heat."

Isaiah 25:4

Chalk It Up

"Personal worth is not something human beings are free to take or leave. We must have it and when it is unattainable, everyone suffers."

–Dr. James Dobson

"There is no greater challenge than teaching a troubled child. If you're willing to be creative, to risk, to try and fail and try again, working with a troubled child can teach you more and touch you more deeply than any other encounter."

–L. Tobin

Lesson Plan

Too often it becomes easy to lose yourself in the quagmire of paperwork that is required from teachers. Lesson plans, daily assignments to correct, local assessments, permanent files, referrals to special education, notes to parents, notes from parents and behavior reports. As necessary as all this paper pushing has become for the functioning of schools, our real job is to reach out and touch the lives of the students in our class. Change them for today. Change them for eternity. Don't get buried alive today in paperwork. Spend some quality time with your students. That's why we all became teachers.

PASSING THE TORCH

My husband and I attended the Meiners' Family Reunion for the first and last time. We live too far to make it an annual affair. Leaning across the family reunion picnic table, a cousin, Charlotte, drawled, "I met a former teacher of yours. From Sherman No. 7 School. Mrs.Mae Erie. She heard my name was Meiners and she found me in the crowd. Wanted to know what happened to 'those two blonde-haired Meiners girls'."

"What did you tell her?" I asked.

"Well, I told her that you and your sister went to school at Sherman. But, you had moved to another state and our families never kept in contact."

My second and third grade teacher not only remembered, but had asked about me thirty years later. The thought seemed astonishing, but one-room country schools in central Iowa didn't boast high mobility rates. Having the same farm families for an entire career, a teacher gets to know her students. My sister and I attended Sherman No. 7 for only two years. But I suspect we typified the pupils who become memorable.

We had to be easy to remember because we wore clothes made from feed sack material. A chic clothing alternative for poverty stricken migrant workers of the Depression, but not the choice for mid-1950 dressmakers. My mom handstitched the smocking, used recycled homemade lace, then stitched embroidery to design "one of a kind" creations. We wore them with pride. Mrs. Erie probably noticed our clothes because she gave me her daughter's outgrown coat for the winter.

My sister and I were hard to forget because we lived in an uninsulated chicken house. Not a used one. A new one, until a house could be moved onto the premises. Mom glued newspapers to the walls to keep the icy windows from blowing through and hung sheets from the rafters for walls. We carried water from the well and drank from a dipper, after scooping the drowned flies from the surface. Winters were spent huddled around a wood burning stove, singing songs, telling stories, or listening to the radio. Orange crates served as dressers, end tables and cupboards.

Maybe Mrs. Erie recalled us because my stepfather drank a lot. Midcentury was a time when domestic violence did not have a name, only cuts and bruises. We never talked about the violence we endured, but the evidence on our bodies spoke clearly

Searching the Internet, my sister found Mrs. Erie's address in a nursing home nestled in the small city near the country school where she had taught for thirty years. I wrote to her so she would know that we remembered her warmth as a teacher and that both my sister and I are educators with Master's degrees. Several weeks later, a letter from Nebraska arrived from Mrs. Erie's daughter.

"She has dementia, but I read your letter to Mom every time I visit. Enclosed are two photographs of yourself and your sister. They have been in our family album for years.

Mom would want you to have them. I feel I have always known you." Mrs. Erie's daughter closed the letter with love. I felt like a guardian angel had been watching over me all these years.

The fact that Mae Erie asked about "those blonde-haired Meiners girls" haunts me. Countless students have sat in my classes whose names have vanished from my memory. Yet, there are some children who never leave my consciousness. They sit on the edge of remembrance and tug at my heart at the strangest times, at unguarded moments.

I think often of former students. Tony, who murdered a rival gang member at age fifteen and languishes in prison. George, whose recovery from being a crack cocaine baby as he finishes high school astounds us. Bobby, who I visited in a psych ward and will undoubtedly be in and out of mental institutions all his life. Crystal, the elective mute who never spoke in class, but accidentally answered me on the phone and couldn't forgive herself. Many others fade in and out of remembrance.

Like Mae Erie, I pray for these young adults when they enter my mind. Maybe, someday, before dementia sets in on me, they will contact me and tell me how well they are doing. How they have become "diamonds from the tough."

Look It Up

"But we also rejoice in our suffering, because we know that suffering produces perseverance; perseverance, character, and character, hope."

Romans 5:3–4

"Her children arise and call her blessed."

Proverbs 31:28

"I have no greater joy than to hear that my children are walking in the truth."

3 John 4

Chalk It Up

"I have never regretted the time spent with a child. It is an investment in eternity."

Cleo Lampos

"I expect to pass through this world but once; any good thing therefore that I can do, or any kindness that I can show to any fellow creature, let me do it now, for I shall not pass this way again."

–Etienne De Grellet

Lesson Plan

Every year a new group of challenges strut into our classroom. Kids with chips on their shoulders and a dare to knock them off. Others who hunch in their sweatshirts and pull the hoods over their heads. The lonely. The shy. The hurt. The smart aleck. Lots of rough edges that need gentle polishing, for underneath it all is a priceless human soul. A diamond in the tough.

Epilogue

Now that you have read **Teaching Diamonds in the Rough,** you probably have a story of your own that needs to be shared. It would be my privilege to present your vignette on my website. Write the details in a story format of 350 words more or less. A favorite quote or Scripture at the end adds to the emphasis of your words. Send your story to *clampos@sbcglobal.net*. You will be informed when your work will appear in the guest column of my website.

References

Melissa's Gift
Gary Chapman and Ross Campbell, *Five Love Languages for Children* (Chicago: Northfield, 1997), page 54

Lock Down
Gary Chapman and Ross Campbell, *Five Love Languages for Children* (Chicago: Northfield, 1997), page 137

Mourning Dove's Cry
Mary McLeod Bethune, Edited by Audrey Thomas McClusky and Elaine M. Smith, *Building a Better World*, (Bloomington and Indianapolis: Indiana University Press, 1999), page 52.

Jane Rubietta-*Quiet Places* (Minneapolis, Minnesota: Bethany House Publishers, 1996), page 65.

Wonderful Wednesday

Edited by Pamela Espeland, *Making the Most of Today*, (Minneapolis, Minnesota: Free Spirit Publishing, Inc., 1991), page 43.

Explosive Situation

Jacqueline Sweeney, *Incredible Quotations*, (New York, NY: Scholastic, Inc., 1997), page 42.

Dog Eared Books

Booker T. Washington, *Up From Slavery* (New York: Bantam Pathfinder Edition, 1900, reprinted March, 1970), page 53.

Known By Name

Justin Kaplan and Ann Baernays-*The Language of Names*, (New York, NY: Simon and Schuster, 1997), page 213.

Benjamin and Elaine Bleck-*Your Name Is A Blessing*, (Northvale, New Jersey: Jason Aronson, Inc, 1999), page 4.

Joseph Bruchac, *Boy Called Slow-A Boy Named Slow*, (New York: Philomel Books, 1994), page 13.

What Johnny Saw

Gary Chapman and Ross Campbell, *Five Love Languages of Children*, (Chicago: Northfield, 1997), page 47

Frank Peretti, *Wounded Spirit*, (Nashville: Word Publishing, A Nelson Thomas Company, 2000), page 155.

Jaqueline Sweeney, *Incredible Quotations*, (New York, NY: Scholastic, Inc., 1997), page16.

Sign of the Star

David Wilkerson with John and Elizabeth Sherrill, *The Cross and the Switchblade*, (New Jersey: A Spire Book, published by Jove Publications, Inc. for Fleming H. Revell, Old Tappan, 1964), page 51.

Sleepless Nights and Secure Days

Gary Chapman and Ross Campbell, *Five Love Languages of Children*, (Chicago: Northfield, 1997) page 140.

Cup of Cold Water

Gary Chapman and Ross Campbell, *Five Love Languages of Children*, (Chicago: Northfield, 1997), page 141.

Kathyrn Stockett, *The Help*, (Amy Einhon Books/G.P. Putnam's Sons, 2010).

And To All a Good Night

Frank Peretti, *Wounded Spirit* (Nashville: Word Publishing, A Thomas Nelson Company. 2000), page183.

Alcoholics Anonymous, *Twelve Steps and Twelve Traditions* (Alcoholics Anonymous World Services, Inc. Fiftieth printing, 1994), pages 5–6.

From Different Eyes

Thank You To . . . My Teacher (Grand Rapids, Michigan: Compiled by Family Christian Press, 2006), page 30.

Hidden Treasures

Fran Durbin, Primary teacher for Cook County District 130 in Illinois. Auditory quote with permission to use.

Macolm's Story
L.Tobin, *What Do You Do With a Child Like This? Inside the Lives of Troubled Children* (Duluth, Minnesota: Whole Person Associates, 1991), page 20 and 18.

To the Other Mother
Debbie Salter Goodwin, "Standing in the Gap," *Adoption Blessings*, Volume 4, 2001, page 2.

Jody Moreen, "On Being Adopted," *Adoption Blessings*, Volume 7, 2003, page 5.

The Untouchable
James Dobson, *Hide Or Seek*,. (Old Tappan, New Jersey: Fleming H. Revell Company, 1971), page 13.

L. Tobin, *What Do You Do With a Child Like This? Inside the Lives of Troubled Children* (Duluth, Minnesota: Whole Person Associates, 1991), page 204.

Passing the Torch
John Bartlett, *Familiar Quotations*, (Boston and Toronto: 14th Edition, Little, Brown and Company, 1882, 1871, 1968), page 531.

Made in the USA
Lexington, KY
23 November 2012